To:

- - - - - - - - - - - - - - -

From:

- - - - - - - - - - - - - - -

The Gospel
According to
Dogs

Also by Robert L. Short

The Gospel According to Peanuts

The Gospel from Outer Space

The Parables of Peanuts

Short Meditations on the Bible and Peanuts

Something to Believe In

A Time to Be Born—A Time to Die

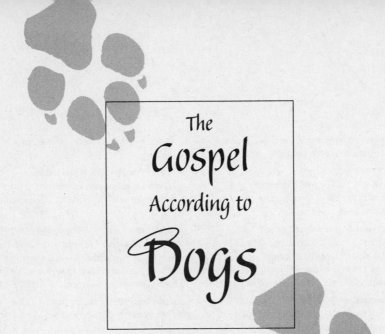

The Gospel According to Dogs

What Our Four-Legged Saints Can Teach Us

ROBERT L. SHORT

HarperSanFrancisco
A Division of HarperCollinsPublishers

FIRST EDITION

Library of Congress Cataloging-in-Publication Data is available upon request.

ISBN: 978–0–06–119874–8
ISBN-10: 0–06–119874–9

07 08 09 10 11 CW 10 9 8 7 6 5 4 3 2 1

For "Sparky" Schulz—How we miss him!

If it is for this life only

that Christ has given us hope,

we of all people are most to be pitied.

1 CORINTHIANS 15:19 (REB)

Introductory Yelp

JESUS, in attempting to get people's attention and also in attempting to make himself clear once their attention was got, would often use similes. He would say, "The kingdom of heaven is like ..." and then he'd go on to say just that—what the kingdom of heaven was like. Using images in parable, comparison, and simile, Jesus would "show" us (Luke 6:47) a picture that in some way resembled his Father's kingdom: "The kingdom of heaven is like a mustard seed" (Matthew 13:31); "the kingdom of heaven is like yeast that a woman took and mixed in with three measures of flour until all of it was leavened" (Matthew 13:33); "the kingdom of heaven is like treasure hidden in a field" (Matthew 13:44); "the kingdom of heaven is like a merchant in search of fine pearls" (Matthew 13:45).

In using cartoons in my books, I'm trying to do the same two things—to get people's attention and then also to make clear my own take on the meaning of Jesus. I'm not trying to interpret the cartoon or tell you what was in the mind of the cartoonist. For anyone to claim they know what is in the mind of another person is not only presumptuous but impossible. Shakespeare was always warning us about this kind of thing. For instance, there's a semi-comic scene in *Richard III* in which the Bishop of Ely asks Buckingham if he knows what Richard is thinking. Buckingham replies:

Who, I, my lord! We know each other's faces,

But for our hearts, he knows no more of mine

Than I of yours—

Nor I no more of his than you of mine. (III, iv, 10–13)

So I just want to be clear that in this book I'm not at all intending to say what any cartoonist intended. I'm only attempting to say what I think the person of Jesus intends. The cartoons I'm using should only be seen as beautiful little pearl-like illustrations. The kingdom of heaven is like when Red says to Rover …; it is like Snoopy when he …; it is like Daisy's love of …; etc. These are similes, mere similes, and in no way am I attempting to read the mind of any cartoonist. Sometimes it's hard enough for me to know what I'm thinking myself without trying to guess what's going on in anyone else's head.

And I'll be doggoned if this isn't so!

I've had a lot of kind and generous help in putting this little book together. In particular I'd like to thank Monte Schulz, Charles M. "Sparky" Schulz's older son, who, since his dad passed away, graciously initiated a friendship that fills a lot of the large empty place left in my life by Sparky's absence. I hope I've done something of the same for Monte. Indeed, the Charles Schulz family as a whole are very gracious to allow me to use the *Peanuts* strips in this "dog tract,"[1] and for that I sincerely thank them. Also, special thanks to Kim Towner of Charles M. Schulz Creative Associates. At Harper San Francisco, Kris Ashley and my most excellent editor Cindy DiTiberio have turned out to be the best of friends. As for my Little Rock friend Ron Wolfe (truly the best-natured wolf anyone could ever hope to know), I'm sure his *Christian Dogma by Karl Bark* cartoon will bring as much delight to many others as it has to me. During the whelping time of this unruly little puppy, "eye hath not heard, ear hath not seen, nor tongue conceived" (as the Pauline Bottom would put it)[2] how much the lovely Alice Buckley has helped, especially in her cheerful mastery of a complete mystery to me, the Internet. (In Samuel Beckett's 1954 play *Waiting for Godot*, Pozzo says of the Christ-figure Lucky, "He thinks he's entangled in a net." I'm sure I'd think the same thing if this old dog were to try this new trick.) And as for the many friendly audiences who have seen the core of this book presented in the form of a color slide program, their nourishing comments and encouragement have made these get-togethers for me personally what suppertimes are for Snoopy—"joyous occasions."

R.L.S.

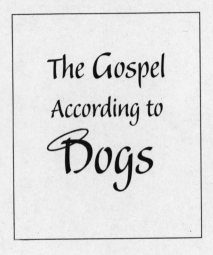

The Gospel
According to
Dogs

"IF ANYONE is in Christ," says St. Paul, "he is a new creature" (2 Corinthians 5:17, RSV). "It does not matter at all whether or not one is circumcised," says Paul; "what does matter is being a new creature" (Galatians 6:15, GNB). Okay, so Christians are "new creatures." But just exactly what kind of "new creatures" have they become? They're now dogs. Jesus makes this clear when a Canaanite—that is, a "canine-ite"—woman falls at his feet. This woman is dogging the footsteps of Jesus and his disciples and making a complete nuisance of herself (Matthew 15:21–28). "Send her away," the disciples say, "for she keeps shouting after us" (v. 23). So Jesus turns to her and says, "I was sent only to the lost sheep of the house of Israel" (v. 24). Does this stop her? Not even almost. "But she came and knelt before him," Matthew tells us (v. 25). Get the picture? If not, Rembrandt, with one of his drawings of this scene, can help us see what happened. Evidently, for Rembrandt, as for Martin Luther, "the Canaanite woman was a source of unending wonder and comfort."[3]

This dog of a woman—for so the Canaanites were thought of by the Jews, especially the Canaanite women—this Canaanite dog was quite willing to play this part, to become a dog, literally down on all fours. Literally begging. Not only a Canaanite and a woman, but now also a dog! How low can a person sink? "Lord, help me," she cries. Then Jesus gives her

Drawing by Rembrandt. Courtesy of Albertina Vienna.

the ultimate test: "It is not fair to take the children's food and throw it to the dogs," he tells her. "Yes, Lord," she answers, "yet even the dogs eat the crumbs that fall from their masters' table" (vv. 26–27). That does it! That is the answer Jesus wants to hear. In the single place in scripture where Jesus seems to have changed his mind, he says, "'Woman, great is your faith! Let it be done for you as you wish.' And her daughter was healed instantly" (v. 28).

This was nothing new in the ministry of Jesus. From the very beginning he'd been consistent and insistent that his message was directed to the spiritually poor, to the lowest of the low in heart, to emotional down-and-outers, to those knocked down on all fours, to those who were willing to crawl—to the dogs, in other words. And here she came, taking Jesus at his word, groveling and grateful for any little scrap that might fall from his table. She became a dog. And this was exactly the kind of humility Jesus was looking for. Now she was no longer a Canaanite, and certainly she was not a Jew.

She was a new creature: she was now a disciple of Jesus—she was now a dog.

And so it is that the dog has become a traditional representation for faith in Christian symbolism. For instance, we're told that "the dog, because of his watchfulness and fidelity, has been accepted as the symbol of these virtues."[4] And that "black-and-white dogs were sometimes used as symbols of the Dominicans (*Domini canes*, "dogs of the Lord") who wore black-and-white habits."[5]

In Christian teaching—Christian "dogma"—Christ is seen as the doorway to God, and the doorway to belief in Christ is understood as humility, the cross, the renunciation or letting go of whatever goals or ultimate concerns we have previously served and lived for. In this letting go, our hands and arms are stretched wide open, just as Christ's were as he hung on the cross. But whether we are emotionally stretched out to the breaking point or we metaphorically fall on all fours, as the Canaanite woman did, this infinitely low point of suffering is the necessary first step in becoming a real Christian. This is the first reason all real Christians are dogs. At the beginning of our journey, each one of us was knocked down to this doglike level of lowliness. It's precisely from this lowest of low points that Christ originally raised us up. It was at rock bottom that we finally found the rock-firm foundation that we needed. It's only out of these depths that real faith can be born—to humbly follow and cry after Jesus as "Lord!"

This is why children have also been seen as a New Testament symbol for what it means to be a Christian. Like dogs, kids can exhibit the same qualities of humility and willingness to learn and to obey. Their lowliness puts them on the same close-to-the-floor spiritual level:

"That's why dogs like little kids.
Grown-ups' faces are out of reach."

Family Circus © Bill Keane, Inc. King Features Syndicate

Therefore, take care if you don't like dogs. This dislike can be a sign of a deeper spiritual malady. The story goes that

> Martin Luther played with his dog and said, "The dog is a very faithful animal and is held in high esteem if he isn't too ordinary. Our Lord God has made the best gifts most common.... But we don't acknowledge such everyday gifts. We are stupid clods."[6]

Peanuts, © United Feature Syndicate, Inc.

Just because of their love, their natural kindness, dogs can go a long way in helping humankind to live up to this word. This is why Dostoevsky said that children should be raised with a dog or a cow or a horse. But cows don't always come when you call them, and horses are too messy in the house. Therefore, like Red in Brian Basset's *Red and Rover,* I would personally prefer someone more like Rover.

Red and Rover, © 2002, The Washington Post Writers Group

"God's kindness," says the Apostle Paul, "is meant to lead you to a change of heart" (Romans 2:4, NEB)—a change that enables you to be kinder to yourself and to others. The kindness of dogs can do the same.

Paul also advised Christians to "hold to the standard of sound teaching that you have heard from me" (2 Timothy 1:13). For Christians, of course, the ultimate "standard of sound teaching" is Christ himself. But in the meantime, our love for dogs is not only a good indicator of what all of us really want and need, but also a good standard for understanding what Christ actually gives us and the kind of Christians we should therefore try to be.

Bizarro, © Dan Piraro. King Features Syndicate

But to say that there is a deep resemblance between dogs and Christians doesn't necessarily mean that Christians should *own* dogs. Christians just need to own up to all the ways in which dogs can be good role models for them. Jesus himself probably never owned a dog. In any case, this is a question that doesn't really have an answer and doesn't really need one.

Peanuts, © United Feature Syndicate, Inc.

Furthermore—

Peanuts, © United Feature Syndicate, Inc.

One other question: are we talking about a particular kind of dog, or are we just talking about ...

Peanuts, © United Feature Syndicate, Inc.

Any dog because all dogs have marvelously magnificent qualities in common with Christians, regardless of what breed of dog or Christian we're talking about—as we can see in this *Classic Mother Goose & Grimm.*

Classic Mother Goose & Grimm, © GRIMMY, INC. King Features Syndicate

But exactly what are these qualities we're talking about? Surely the analogy between dogs and Christians doesn't stop with the humility with which they both eat the scraps that fall from their masters' table. If there's more, what are some of the specifics?

First, there is *obedience.* Christians are not really Christians unless they obey their Master. How could anyone claim that Jesus is their Lord unless they actually obeyed the commands of this Lord? And dogs are legendary for their obedience. But this common obedience of Christians and dogs doesn't come easily for either. It is said of Christ that "son though he was, he learned obedience in the school of suffering" (Hebrews 5:8, NEB). Christians and dogs must all go to the same school. And guess which of these students makes the more difficult pupil! In the Bible, severe estimations are often made of humankind that are not made of the other animals. For instance, Paul can say of all the Christians among "man": "We ourselves were once foolish, disobedient, led astray, slaves to various passions and pleasures" (Titus 3:3). For just this reason Paul saw that the first thing needed by all humankind was the new "obedience school" opened by Christ, an obedience school much like the one Helga looks forward to in *Hagar*.

Hagar the Horrible, © King Features Syndicate

The job of both Christians and dogs is to provide the world with protection and comfort, love, joy and companionship.

This is what it means to obey God and to have faith in him. But again, no one ever said this job would be easy for either dogs or Christians:

Peanuts, © United Feature Syndicate, Inc.

And so then, dogs and Christians share in "the obedience of love" (see, for example, 1 Peter 1:22). Ordinarily we think of love as something we only *feel.* But Christians and canines know that love is something we also *do,* regardless of how we may feel. Love—Christian love—is something we *do* or it isn't really Christian love. Love—Christian love—is a love that intends to actually help. And the kind of love we are talking about—Christian love (the New Testament's *agape*)—aims at being as much as possible a faithful reflection of *God's* love. That is, it must be unconditional love, a love that knows no limits. Sad to say, we can more often find instances of this kind of love in dogs than in people. In *Pickles,* Nelson's grandfather tells him:

Pickles, © 1999, The Washington Post Writers Group

The poet Rainer Maria Rilke wrote:

> God … sat down for a moment when the dog was finished to
> watch it … and to know it was good, that nothing was lacking,
> that it could not have been made better.[7]

Similarly, there's this well-known statement by George Graham Vest:

*"The one absolutely unselfish friend that
man can have in this selfish world is his dog."*[8]

27

Obedience to God also means total *Dependence on God* (DOG) and not finally depending on ourselves. And here again, the dog is a marvelous model for Christian faith. Just as dogs are totally dependent on their master, so real Christians are totally dependant on theirs. Christians—and this is why they are called "Christ-ians"—do what they do with their "eyes fixed on Jesus, on whom faith depends from start to finish" (Hebrews 12:2, NEB). If Christians were to mistakenly believe that the start of their faith depends on their own free decisions for Christ, then obviously they'd be depending on themselves from the very beginning, not on Christ. In this way, all such trust in ourselves undercuts all trust in God. We become *self*-righteous instead of depending on "God and *his* righteousness" (Matthew 6:33). We become our own saviors.This is why Paul is careful to make clear that it is "by the grace of God I am what

I am" (1 Corinthians 15:10). Real Christians no more attribute the deep change of their conversion to their own decision or free will than a dog thinks it freely decided to be born a dog. It is by forces totally outside themselves that they have become what they have become. Otherwise, they'd have a basis for boasting or pride. It is only by the grace of God that they are what they are. The choice was not theirs. Someone else had already done the choosing: "You did not choose me but I chose you," said Jesus to his special "friends" (John 15:16).

Peanuts, © United Feature Syndicate, Inc.

Genuine Christian conversion is such a deep and profound experience that earlier ages of faith even coined a phrase— "the perseverance of the saints"—for the realization that once it has happened in a person's life, there's no going back on it. Jesus was pointing to this reality when he compared Christian conversion to being "born again" (John 3:3, 7 REB)—that is, conversion is just as deeply affecting as our births themselves, which also were not our doing. Now, however, the Christian experiences an entirely new birth that has an infinitely more satisfying orientation, and therefore the Christian experiences a doglike, persevering love that finally cannot be diverted. Christians become *hounds* for Christ. They are now "locked in" to Christ. And so Jesus could say of his own "retrievers": "My Father who has given them to me is greater than all, and no one can snatch them out of the Father's care" (John 10:29, REB). This might be called the "divine tenacity": when we fully realize that God is never going to let us go, then we never want to let God go.

Peanuts, © United Feature Syndicate, Inc.

But in the lives of Christians, so also in the lives of dogs: "obedience to" always means "faith in." The two can't be separated. I don't think anyone has ever understood this better than Dietrich Bonhoeffer:

> *Only he who believes is obedient, and only he who is obedient believes.* ... For faith is only real where there is obedience, never without it, and faith only becomes faith in the act of obedience. (emphasis Bonhoeffer's)[9]

Faith is the love affair the heart has with the resurrected Jesus. Faith needs no other object than this. Love needs only the loved one to know its love is true. It needs no other proofs or props; indeed, if they were available, the proofs or props would actually be what was most loved or trusted. For this reason, God does not demand that we *know* him, but only that we have *faith* in him—that we *love* him. Knowledge is being convinced by our eyes, by what we can see. Faith and love are being convinced by our hearts. This is why Paul can say, "We walk by faith, not by sight" (2 Corinthians 5:7).

Faith and sight represent two radically different ways of understanding Christian faith and the Christian church. In one, Christian faith's love of the crucified and resurrected Christ is all that's needed: "For I decided to know nothing among you except Jesus Christ," Paul said, "and him crucified" (1 Corinthians 2:2). In the other, all sorts of additional reasons, proofs, and supports are thought to be necessary. But in this case, "the additional," whatever it might be, becomes an idol or false god, a diversion from the true God. When Jesus was stripped at the time of his crucifixion, this was a way of saying that precisely here—in no one else and in nothing else—was the one who must be believed and obeyed. But people and churches are embarrassed by the nakedness and isolation of this man and quickly attempt to cover him with all sorts of additional things, things that are more respectable and impressive in one way or another. *Christian faith* is always totally satisfied with the love it receives from its humble God—its "dog God." *Christianity,* on the other hand, always wants more.

Red and Rover, © 2002, The Washington Post Writers Group

This is why faith always catches the greatest number of fish, not among people who already have plenty, but, strange to say, in the dry and desert regions—as happens with Winslow, the little coyote (or "desert dog") in Scott Stantis's *Prickly City,* or as Jesus does in the gospels when the crowds, hearing that he and the disciples have gone away to "a deserted place," congregate there in great numbers. Then Jesus, seeing that they are hungry, "had compassion for them, because they were like sheep without a shepherd" (Mark 6:31–44). There fish are found in abundance. Sheep, dogs, and fish—all New Testament symbols for faith.

Prickly City, © 2005 Scott Stantis. Distributed by Universal Press Syndicate

Faith is quite happy just to have faith. It already has the joy it was always seeking. It doesn't need to become anything else; it couldn't be anything better. In one of the last letters that Dietrich Bonhoeffer wrote before he was hanged by the Nazis, he finally realized that he would probably not survive the war but would soon be put to death because of his part in attempting to assassinate Hitler. In this letter he writes to his closest friend:

> I remember a conversation that I had in America thirteen years ago with a young French pastor. We were asking ourselves quite simply what we wanted to do with our lives. He said he would like to become a saint (and I think it's quite likely that he did become one). At the time I was very impressed, but I disagreed with him, and said, in effect, that I should like to learn to have faith. For a long time I didn't realize the depth of the contrast. I thought I could acquire faith by trying to live a holy life, or something like it.... I discovered later, and I'm still discovering right up to this moment, that it is only by living completely in this world

that one learns to have faith. One must completely abandon any attempt to make something of oneself, whether it be a saint, or a converted sinner, or a churchman (a so-called priestly type!), a righteous man or an unrighteous one, a sick man or a healthy one. By this-worldliness I mean living un-reservedly in life's duties, problems, successes and failures, experiences and perplexities. In so doing we throw ourselves completely into the arms of God, taking seriously, not our own sufferings, but those of God in the world—watching with Christ in Gethsemane. That, I think, is faith;... and that is how one becomes a man and a Christian. How can success make us arrogant, or failure lead us astray, when we share in God's sufferings through a life of this kind?

I think you see what I mean, even though I put it so briefly. I'm glad to have been able to learn this, and I know I've been able to do so only along the road that I've traveled. So I'm grateful for the past and present, and content with them.[10]

Mother Goose & Grimm © GRIMMY, INC. King Features Syndicate

But there are other reasons why dogs can be seen as appropriate symbols for Christian faith. For instance,

F. R. Maltby once said, "Jesus promised his disciples three things—that they would be completely fearless, absurdly happy, and in constant trouble."[11]

So, are these three alleged attributes of Christians also characteristically canine? For example, are dogs absurdly happy? Yes! And why is that? Well, first of all, they only care about the things that really matter. What a marvelous freedom this gives them! For example, do you think they really care about who wins some silly game? Of course not! They just enjoy being with their friends.

Peanuts, © United Feature Syndicate, Inc.

On a huge billboard in downtown Los Angeles I once saw a picture of a sleeping puppy with a simple caption beside it: "Dogs rule." And so they do. They are not slaves to the things of this world. They are slaves only of their master, and their master, like that of Christians, has already conquered the world—not *will* conquer it, but has *already* conquered it. "I have told you all this," said Jesus,

... so that in me you may find peace. In the world you will have trouble. But courage! The victory is mine; I have conquered the world. (John 16:33, NEB)

Said Paul:

If God is for us, who is against us? He who did not withhold his own Son, but gave him up for all of us, will he not with him also give us everything else?... No, in all these things we are more than conquerors through him who loved us. (Romans 8:31–32, 37)

"Happy are those who claim nothing," said Jesus, "for the whole earth will belong to them" (Matthew 5:5, J. B. Phillips translation). This is why dogs, like Christians, are absurdly happy. This is also why they rule.

Greg Evans's popular comic strip *Luann* is about a fairly typical high school teen who is always trying to understand why she's not happier. So Luann and her dog, Puddles, pay a visit to Mrs. Horner, a neighbor and a mentor to Luann. Mrs. Horner wisely observes that self-centeredness is often the cause of unhappiness. And then the conversation goes like this:

Luann, © GEC Inc./Distributed by United Feature Syndicate, Inc.

Luann, © GEC Inc./Distributed by United Feature Syndicate, Inc.

So dogs live happily by faith and love. But they also live by *hope.* That is, they also have something to look forward to. Their lives are not ultimately meaningless—which their lives would be if they were going to end up only in the grave.

Peanuts, © United Feature Syndicate, Inc.

"Everyone?" *Absolutely everyone* is going to heaven! And not only everyone, but also *everything*—including all dogs, of course. And the person and the event that made this final outcome sure and certain is a done deal. It's already happened:

> Through (Christ) God chose to reconcile the whole universe to himself, making peace through the shedding of his blood upon the cross—to reconcile all things, whether on earth or in heaven, through him alone. (Colossians 1:20, NEB)

45

Peanuts, © United Feature Syndicate, Inc.

Earl, the little dog in *Mutts,* is right: "Dogs think every day is Christmas." By coming into the world as a particular person on a particular day, God has declared his solidarity with all of us and his undefeatable love for *every* day, for *every* person, for *all* of his creation. By faith in the born and crucified and resurrected Jesus, Christians are convinced absolutely that "in Christ God was reconciling the world to himself, not counting their trespasses against them" (2 Corinthians 5:19). And so Christians and dogs look happily to the future. "In the future life we'll see them," Luther said of dogs.[12]

But in the meantime, Christians and dogs are also absurdly happy because they've been given plenty of meaningful work to do for their Master—who "has given us the ministry of reconciliation" (2 Corinthians 5:18). As much as possible,

"OL' RUFF LIKES EVERYBODY...
EVEN MR. WILSON."

Dennis the Menace, © Used by permission of Hank Ketcham
Enterprises and © North America Syndicate

they are to fill the world with *love*. And it's just *in* this love, this obedience, that they not only love their Master but also know of his love for them. Therefore, dogs can hardly love enough, as in the case of *Dennis the Menace*'s Ruff on the opposite page.

From a practical point of view, all of this emphasis on love and where and how to find it may make Christians and dogs seem to be completely *useless*. What do they *do* with their lives? Quite simply, they point. If Christians had to be a particular type of dog, they'd all be pointers. They "stick to the point"—to the "whole point" of Christianity, which is to find in Christ "the still point of the turning world," as T. S. Eliot wrote.[13] For Christians, everything besides Jesus is "beside the point." To have missed him is to have "missed the point."

Without him, all life is finally "pointless." With him, the meaning of life is "clear and to the point." While resting peacefully on the firm foundation of the witness of the New Testament church (the doghouse), they point constantly upward and so give lessons to everyone in the turning, troubled world on how to find the peace and rest and love they've been looking for. Christians show everyone the calm confidence that comes from having the proper vertical orientation:

Peanuts, © United Feature Syndicate, Inc.

> Unless the Lord builds the house,
>
> those who build it labor in vain.
>
> Unless the Lord guards the city,
>
> the guard keeps watch in vain.
>
> It is in vain that you rise up early
>
> and go late to rest,
>
> eating the bread of anxious toil;
>
> for he gives sleep to his beloved. (Psalm 127:1–2)

Snoopy would agree.

Of course, there are many other types of dogs that Christians can be compared to: guide dogs, guard dogs, therapy dogs, trouble-sniffing dogs, rescue dogs, retrievers, etc. But they're all essentially pointers. That is, the many types of work that Christians do all finally aim at one thing: to point not to themselves or to their work, but to their Master. Martin Luther said that the entire Christian life can be summed up in this command: "To this man [Christ] shalt thou point and say, 'Here is God.'"[14] Christians are called "Christ-ians" because that's exactly what Christians *do*—in their every word and deed. And as far as I'm concerned, that's also what Snoopy is doing in the previous *Peanuts* cartoon.

When Jesus called Christians "the salt of the earth" (Matthew 5:13), he meant that just as salt was the essential preservative of food in the ancient world, likewise Christians *preserve* the earth—it is faith in him that will preserve the entire world from the dissolution of despair and chaos and spiritual malnutrition. Apart from his good news, Jesus knew the world would finally be subject to nothing but the decay of doom and gloom. Fred Basset can see from the daily newspaper that this is the usual way of the world. But he also knows that this same newspaper contains one more small element, just a pinch, namely *him, Fred Basset,* this unconquerably happy comic strip about a dog who—like salt and like faith in Christ, with powers out of all proportion to their size—can always be relied on to cheer us up. For salt not only preserves, exactly as faith does, but also adds zest to our lives. Therefore, it's not at all inappropriate that Paul's directive to "let your speech always be gracious, seasoned with salt" (Colossians 4:6), can also be translated as "always talk pleasantly and with a flavor of wit" (NJB).

A Christian has every reason to be happy, and that happiness is well expressed by an old hymn that tells us:

> What a wonderful change in my life has been wrought
> Since Jesus came into my heart!
> I have light in my soul for which long I had sought,
> Since Jesus came into my heart!
> Since Jesus came into my heart,
> Floods of joy o'er my soul like the sea billows roll,
> Since Jesus came into my heart.[15]

That happiness is also well expressed by this *Red and Rover* cartoon:

Red and Rover, © 2002, The Washington Post Writers Group

No wonder *Time* magazine can report that "heart-failure patients fare much better—with lower anxiety and stress-hormone scores—when visited in the hospital by dogs rather than people" (November 28, 2005).

So dogs and Christians are both absurdly happy, to go back to Maltby's way of putting it. And faith, hope, and love all play their parts in making this so. "And the greatest of these is love" (1 Corinthians 13:13). This, of course, is finally because God himself "is love" (1 John 4:8). But we must never discount the power that *hope* has in bringing happiness to the world. Insofar as men and women live without the certainty that they will finally be with God after they die, their lives—logically—are ultimately quite hopeless. And the inevitable effect of this hopelessness is the desperate selfishness of brute beasts. "Just let me get mine while the getting's good!"

Brian Anderson, the cartoonist who draws *Dog Eat Doug*, is a great fan of dogs, and also apparently a fan of the nineteenth-century British novelist Maria Louise "Ouida" Ramée, who was herself famous for her love of animals in general and dogs in particular. In one of his cartoons, Anderson has the dog of his strip, Sophie, quote from Ouida:

Dog Eat Doug, © Brian Anderson and Creators Syndicate, Inc.

"Take hope from the heart of man," all you atheists, agnostics, humanists, and believers in a God of hell (where, as Dante would say, there is no hope), and you will make of this man you supposedly love "a beast of prey."

But are dogs and Christians "completely fearless," as Jesus said his disciples would be? Why shouldn't they be fearless? The Psalmist long ago taught the dogs of Christ that "with the Lord on my side I do not fear" (Psalm 118:6). And as for dogs:

Peanuts, © United Feature Syndicate, Inc.

The dog of Jesus might get tired of walking around in all that sand, but one thing that Christians and dogs can never do is rue the day—that is, despair so deeply that we wish that a particular day (or days) had never been given to us. The deep and abiding assurance within Christians and dogs gives them the knowledge of an infinite love behind all life and all creation. Regardless of how bad things may appear at the moment—and they "may have regret and remorse, and may even experience repentance"—they believe, with Shakespeare, that "the love that follows us sometime is our trouble, / Which still we thank as love" (*Macbeth*, I, vi, 11–12). Or as Paul put it:

> We are afflicted in every way, but not crushed; perplexed, but not driven to despair; persecuted, but not forsaken.
> (2 Corinthians 4:8–9)

And so regret, remorse, and even the experience of repentance can never make Christians rue the day that God has given them. This means, for one thing, that Christians and dogs will be completely fearless in their hounding of idols—or the "blankets" of false gods and false securities.

Peanuts, © United Feature Syndicate, Inc.

So Christians, like dogs, are not cowards. As followers of the Prince of Peace, they are creatures of peace themselves. But armed with fearlessness for their Lord, they are always required to take strong stands for their Lord. This means they'll sometimes be expected to take risks and *fight* for their Lord, just as their Lord has fought for them. Shakespeare beautifully advises Christians about what their attitude toward fighting should be when he says: "Beware / Of entrance to a quarrel; but being in, / Bear't that the opposed may beware of thee" (*Hamlet*, I, iii, 65–67). And as with Christians, so also with dogs. They are not afraid to "fight the good fight" (1 Timothy 6:12), just as Louie, in *Overboard*, is completely fearless of a marauding gang of pirates who have attacked his ship's captain:

Overboard, © 1999 Universal Press Syndicate

But just as there are different types of battles, there are also different types of fear. One of the most disabling forms of fear that afflicts humankind is anxiety—worry and misgivings caused by all of the world's uncertainties. In some of the loveliest and most famous words of the New Testament, Jesus tells us that the origin of this type of fear is misplaced priorities—that is, not understanding what should come *first* in our lives:

Therefore I tell you, do not worry about your life, what you will eat or what you will drink, or about your body, what you will wear. Is not life more than food, and the body more than clothing? Look at the birds of the air; they neither sow nor reap nor gather into barns, and yet your heavenly Father feeds them. Are you not of more value than they? And can any of you by worrying add a single hour to your span of life? And why do you worry about clothing? Consider the lilies of the field, how they grow; they neither toil nor spin, yet I tell you, even Solomon in all his glory was not clothed like one of these. But if God so clothes the grass of the field, which is alive today and tomorrow is thrown into the oven, will he not much more clothe you—you of little faith? Therefore do not worry, saying, "What will we eat?" or "What will we drink?" or "What will we wear?" For it is the Gentiles who strive for all these things; and indeed your heavenly Father knows that you need all these things. But strive first for the kingdom of God and his righteousness, and all these things will be given to you as well. (Matthew 6:25–33)

When confronted by all our problems, our all-too-human response is to take arms against a sea of troubles and oppose them. But the beauty of being a dog is that the dog—like the beautiful birds of the air or the "daisies of the field"—understands what's worth worrying about and what is not:

Blondie, © King Features Syndicate

And finally, as Maltby says, Jesus promised that Christians will be in constant trouble. Is this also true of dogs? Oh, I think so! Christians and dogs are in constant trouble because, if nothing else, they are "troubleshooters." This is literally true of Snoopy, who—in his trusty World War I fighter plane, the "Sopwith Camel"—constantly pursues the infamous and dreaded World War I flying menace, the Red Baron. It's easy to see who the Red Baron represents for Snoopy—an aristocratic archenemy in red with diabolical powers of evil. An apt figure for Satan, "the Prince of Darkness," if there ever was one. "Curse the Red Baron and his kind! Curse the wickedness in this world! Curse the evil that causes all this unhappiness!" shouts Snoopy at the "spiritual forces of evil in the heavenly places" (Ephesians 6:12) after getting shot down by the Red Baron for the umpteenth time.

Charles Schulz was always aware of the salt that he frequently sprinkled on *Peanuts*. And in the many conversations we had over the years, I sometimes could see this too. I know he was fascinated by the passage in the Gospel of Luke in which seventy-two dogs sent out by Jesus return to him:

> The seventy-two came back rejoicing. "Lord," they said, "even the devils submit to us when we use your name." He said to them, "I watched Satan fall like lightning from heaven." ... Just at this time, filled with joy by the Holy Spirit, he said, "I bless you, Father, Lord of heaven and earth, for hiding these things from the learned and the clever, and revealing them to little children." (Luke 10:17, 21, NJB)

This passage spoke so strongly to Sparky Schulz that he learned to quote it from beginning to end. I see three main reasons for his love of it. First, it so clearly proclaims the gospel, "the good news," as he understood the good news: Satan is now done for! He's been shot out of the sky and has fallen "like lightning from heaven." That is, all of the evil that Snoopy curses is now already defeated. The powers of darkness continue to cause trouble, but basically the victory already belongs to Christ. "But thanks be to God, who in Christ always leads us in triumphal procession, and through us spreads in every place the fragrance that comes from knowing him" (2 Corinthians 2:14). Now *everyone*—everywhere—is destined to return to the loving Father from whom they all have come. Satan, hell, death, suffering, evil, and all other "powers of darkness" have already been conquered. Second, God now communicates this message through "little children," just as Schulz communicated what he had to say. Third—and this is a point that used to delight me whenever I heard him talk about it—this is the one place in scripture where it looks as if Jesus might have actually *laughed* ("just at this time" Jesus was "filled with joy by the Holy Spirit"). As a cartoonist and as a dog, Schulz was very interested in this precedent.

Peanuts, © United Feature Syndicate, Inc.

A further point about this cartoon: just as Snoopy is no ordinary dog, the Christian is no ordinary human being, but rather—as we said—a "new creature," one re-created with untold fearlessness and dedication in the face of forbidding darkness and trouble.

The Bible does indeed contain some frightening threats from God about our "naughtiness," another kind of trouble we always get into. For who among us has not been naughty? This is one reason God's salvation turns out to be *universal* salvation. Only a universal salvation can finally be an adequate remedy for so universal a naughtiness. For if God saved only those who were rich in goodness and obedience, "then who," as the "astounded" disciples asked Jesus, "could be saved?" (Matthew 19:25; Mark 10:26; Luke 18:26). That is, if it all came down to a matter of strict justice—of everyone getting exactly what they deserve—then "none of us / Should see salvation," as Shakespeare has Portia say in *The Merchant of Venice* (IV, i, 198–99), echoing the Psalmist's words to God: "Do not enter into judgment with your servant, for no one living is righteous before you" (143:2). We all know from experience that God's bark is plenty unpleasant when it comes, but finally his bark is always much worse than his bite. And here are a couple of examples of how this fortunate fact actually works:

> For a brief moment I abandoned you,
> but with great compassion I will gather you.
> In overflowing wrath for a moment,

I hid my face from you,

but with everlasting love I will have compassion on you,

says the Lord, your Redeemer. (Isaiah 54:7–8)

"Perfect love casts out fear" (1 John 4:18). And what Christians have been given through their faith in Christ is the happy certainty of God's perfect love—his final and "universal restoration of all things" (Acts 3:21; Ephesians 1:10), including dogs.

As Coleridge (himself a good example of someone with this certainty) could have his "Ancient Mariner" conclude:

> He prayeth well who loveth well
> Both man and bird and beast.
> He prayeth best who loveth best
> All things both great and small;
> For the dear God who loveth us,
> He made and loveth all.

There are so many parallels between Christians and dogs that I'll just mention a few more in passing. First, it's the nature of Christians, like dogs, to be *chowhounds*. Christians "hunger and thirst for righteousness" (Matthew 5:6). And so built-in hunger gives both Christians and dogs the one-track minds for which both are so notorious. Charlie Brown never hesitates to get in his digs at Snoopy on this point:

Peanuts, © United Feature Syndicate, Inc.

These "mighty appetites" will always cause dogs and real Christians to have "dedogatory" stones thrown at them:

Peanuts, © United Feature Syndicate, Inc.

Actually, I would think that Snoopy is a dog of *great* depth, since he seems so difficult to fill up. But the point is that if the

Letter of James is right in telling us that "purity of heart is to will one thing" (as the great Dane Søren Kierkegaard translated chapter 4, verse 8),[16] then both dogs and Christians are definitely "pure in heart." Luther also makes this connection:

> When Luther's puppy happened to be at the table, looked for a morsel from his master, and watched with open mouth and motionless eyes, Luther said, "Oh, if I could only pray the way this dog watches the meat! All his thoughts are concentrated in the piece of meat. Otherwise, he has no thought, wish, or hope."[17]

So whether it's Luther's puppy or Louie, the puppy in *Overboard,* or simply a spirit-starved human puppy, doglike hunger will always make them look pretty much the same. Like the Greek searchers for the truth who show up in the Gospel of John, all of their hopes have finally come down to the point of one ravenous wish: "Sir," they said to Philip, "we wish to see Jesus" (John 12:21).

Overboard, © 2003 Universal Press Syndicate

In Mark O'Hare's hilarious comic strip *Citizen Dog,* there's one cartoon in which Mel asks his dog, Fergus, "What's it like to be a dog?" The conversation then proceeds this way:

Citizen Dog © 1997 Mark O'Hare. Distributed by Universal Press Syndicate

There is no doubt that, in a spiritual sense, this *is* a complex question that's difficult to answer and "a difficult thing to pinpoint." Fergus's attempt at an answer, however, comes amazingly close to one of the ways in which this question and its answer are pinpointed by Jesus. And this answer has a lot to do with food. On one occasion after being questioned by his disciples, Jesus sidesteps their curiosity by saying:

Do not work for the food that perishes, but for the food that endures for eternal life, which the Son of Man will give you. For it is on him that God the Father has set his seal.

Of course, this answer immediately raises the counterquestion of exactly what is meant by "work" here. And so it seems that the response to this last question could finally pinpoint what it means to be a dog/Christian. And so it does:

Then they said to him, "What must we do to perform the works of God?" Jesus answered them, "This is the work of God, that you believe in him whom he has sent." (John 6:27–29)

But doesn't believing in Jesus mean believing in the ethical *teachings* of Jesus? No, ultimately it means believing *in him,* Jesus, the divine *teacher.* Without *him* as the teacher, the teachings and all the rest lose all power and authority and finally dwindle into weakness and confusion. And so Kierkegaard said: "It is 1,800 years since Christ lived, so He is forgotten—only His teaching remains—that is to say, Christianity has been done away with."[18] Christians/dogs are those whose hunger has finally been satisfied by *Jesus himself,* "the bread of life" (John 6:48).

Second, the master of a dog always turns out to be a *single flesh-and-blood person.* Dogs don't finally give themselves to abstractions or disembodied ideas, nor to a variety of things, nor even to a variety of people. Their master is their god; "he is one, and besides him there is no other"

(Mark 12:32; Deuteronomy 4:35). Christians are the same way. And mercifully for Christians, in much the same way as it is for dogs, their Master, their one God, "became flesh and lived among us" (John 1:14). Why is this merciful? Why is this an essential part of the "good news"? Because now we know where to find God, as Job said he wished he knew (Job 23:3). In becoming particular and exclusive and specific, the source of all truth and love now comes into clear, settled, unambiguous, and fixed certainty for Christians and for dogs. Shakespeare likens Christ to the North Star, "the star to every wand'ring bark" (sonnet 116). Also, the star to every *wondering* bark. For it's just because of this star's uniqueness, its particularity and exclusivity, that it can guide home an entire wandering, wondering, and perplexed humankind, badly lost at sea in the night. So Christians and dogs are both overjoyed that their master is a specific flesh-and-blood human being. They now know *who* God is. Now there's no need to bark up so many wrong trees. When it was said that the one God had become a real, down-to-earth, single individual and even had a name, Jesus, Christians were people who considered this to be good news indeed. This is why they came to be called "Christians." God was with us in the Garden of Eden, "in the beginning" (Genesis 1:1). But then he seemed to disappear without fully answering all of the questions we had for him. But now, in Jesus—"He's back! He's back! He's back!" Once again God is "Immanuel," that is, "God is with us" (Isaiah 7:14).

Mother Goose & Grimm, © GRIMMY, INC. King Features Syndicate

And just as dogs faithfully follow, look up to, and love their one and only master, so Christians also look up to, love, and faithfully follow theirs. Even—especially!—in the darkest nights of the church's history, even when the point is reached where people seem to be paying little or no attention to their Master, the church itself will always continue to love, look up to, and faithfully pay attention to him. The real church's faith will always be doglike, like Daisy's devotion to Dagwood, and rocklike, like Peter's trust in his Lord. This, as offensively narrow as it might seem to some people, is what it means to "believe":

> Many of his disciples turned back and no longer went about with him. So Jesus asked the twelve, "Do you also wish to go away?" Simon Peter answered him, "Lord, to whom can we go? You have the words of eternal life. We have come to believe and know that you are the Holy One of God." (John 6:66–69)

Dogs and Christians are the people who have correctly identified the master, now dog his steps, and never stop paying the closest attention to him.

Blondie, © King Features Syndicate

Third, it's obvious that dogs, among the animals, are known for their outstanding *intelligence.* And among the various groups within the family of humankind, Christians are likewise supposed to be known for theirs. But is this really true nowadays? Aren't the people called "Christians" more often these days expected to check their minds at the door when they go to church? On the Christian map, on the right-wing side, the conservatives see their job as "holding the Lord in their *hearts*." The liberal side, on the left, feel they've done their work as long as they lend others a *hand*. So when did Christians start neglecting the huge area in between and stop using their *heads*?—often even proud of this fact? When did "faith" start being an excuse for lazy-mindedness and superstitious schlock? When did Christians stop learning and thinking in their service to their Lord? Learning? Thinking?

Yes! For instance, where today do we see dog-eared copies of the Christian constitution, the New Testament, as we so often used to see?

Real faith starts by filling the heart, then spills over into the head, and finally gets the hands moving or it's not really faith. And real faith never tries to make an end run around the head. It has nothing to fear from intelligence. Intelligence—understanding—is faith's best friend. For one thing, if faith really is faith and not soft and simple-minded gullibility, it is always hammered out on the anvil of doubt. For another, wouldn't it be helpful if Christians these days knew and thought far more about history and theology so that they wouldn't be condemned to go on struggling with the same old questions and problems as if these questions and problems were brand-new? If this were the case, then denominational labels, which today have become largely meaningless, might once more stand for something important and recognizable and would no longer be just vague tags for amorphous societies held together mostly by superficial social interests. It no longer matters *which* church we "belong to" only because it no longer matters that much whether we belong to *any* church. But all real Christians are dogs. They hold to their faith doggedly, discerningly, and intelligently. They know what they believe and will defend their own special territory down to its bare bones. Look at the words Paul uses here in addressing the Colossians that point to the work of *a disciple*. Or, as the word *disciple* means, a "learner."

Christ is the master you must serve.... Persevere in prayer, with *minds* alert and with thankful hearts.... Be *wise* in your dealings with outsiders, but use your opportunities to the full.... *Learn* how best to respond to each person you meet. (Colossians 3:24, 4:2, 5–6, REB, emphasis added)

Sounds like Christians are expected to be up on practically everything!

Peanuts, © United Feature Syndicate, Inc.

But dogs not only have an *intelligence* not known among most of the other animals; they also have keen *sensitivities* not even possessed by people. Dogs can hear things people can't hear and smell things people can't smell. These forms of specialized knowledge often make dogs effective "early warning" or "early recognition" systems: they are the first to "smell a rat," and they can often hear their master speaking even when he's nowhere in sight. This is why Karl Barth—surely one of the deepest of all diggers into Christian "dogma" or Christian meaning—can point out that when God asks for "MEN," what he's really asking for is dogs—and not just smart dogs, but dogs of discernment. Barth quotes a German pastor:

God needs MEN, not creatures
Full of noisy, catchy phrases.
Dogs he asks for, who their noses
Deeply thrust into—Today,
And there scent Eternity.

© Ron Wolfe

Barth then goes on to say, "I wish I could be such a Hound of God—*Domini canis*—and could persuade all my readers to enter the Order."[19]

And so the unusual power of perception and discernment found in the dogs of Christ—that is, those who are really collared by Christ—is just one more similarity between ordinary Christians and ordinary dogs. But this is not surprising. Paul long ago prayed that these special ways of knowing would grow in Christians:

> And this is my prayer: that your love may increase ever more and more in knowledge and every kind of perception, to discern what is of value, so that you may be pure and blameless for the day of Christ, filled with the fruit of righteousness that

comes through Jesus Christ for the glory and praise of God. (Philippians 1:9–11, NAB)

Franz Kafka wrote a short story called "Investigations of a Dog," in which—some say—he used dogs to represent Christians. In this story the narrator, himself a dog, says of dogs (or Christians):

> To whom but our own species can one appeal in the wide and empty world? All knowledge, the totality of all questions and all answers is contained in the dog.[20]

This is, of course, a fantastic thing to say about dogs, but it's also hard to believe about Christians. Do Christians really contain "all knowledge, the totality of all questions and all answers"? Are all answers really "contained in the dog"? Is it really Christians—"Christ's body" (Colossians 1:28, REB)—who have "been given to know the secrets of the kingdom of heaven," as Christ could tell his disciples (Matthew 13:11)? And therefore, is it really up to "us," in service to our Master, to bring healing to this wide and empty world? Evidently Paul thought so. Notice how in these statements Paul addresses "us," the entire Christian community of dogs:

God has lavished on us all wisdom and insight. He has made known to us his secret purpose, in accordance with the plan which he determined beforehand in Christ, to be put into effect when the time was ripe: namely, that the universe, everything in heaven, and on earth, might be brought into a unity in Christ. (Ephesians 1:8–10, REB)

To "us"—to us Christians, to us dogs—"has been given to know the secrets of the kingdom of God" (Luke 8:10). What are we going to do with these secrets? Bury them in the back-yard, keep them secret, and thereby deny their truthfulness? In a cowardly, dumbed-down way, are we just going to forget to mention the very center of what Christ came into the world to reveal? That the entire world, "that the universe," everything in heaven and on earth has already been saved and that this is now known by faith in Christ alone? If we do find it inconvenient to make clear this "whole point" of the Christian message, then of course we can always lose our-selves—as we now seem to be lost—in merely the sugar highs of cotton candy Christianity, the sickeningly sweet and sadly superficial spiritual junk food that gives the world balloons when it really needs Jesus "the joy of man's desiring," Jesus "the Savior of the world" (John 4:42). Is this cartoon really an accurate analogy of what our species is doing today?

Peanuts, © United Feature Syndicate, Inc.

Where today do we see Christian communities "lavished with all wisdom and insight" (REB, p. 49)? Are we not rather lavished with fun and games, with busy diversions and distractions, with money and countless other "balloons" and other peripherals that are a long way away from the point, details that wag the dog? Aren't we now dogs that are perfectly content to remain quietly "in front of a fireplace"? But this is the wrong fire and the wrong place: "The more central the message of the church, the greater now will be her effectiveness," said Dietrich Bonhoeffer, pointing clearly to the real place and the real fire.[21] For what is the church's "central message" according to Bonhoeffer? "That God loved the world and reconciled it with Himself in Christ is the central message proclaimed in the New Testament"[22] (see 2 Corinthians 5:18–19; Colossians 1:19–20). Or as Karl Barth said in his monumental *Church Dogmatics:*

> The doctrine of reconciliation is itself the first or last or central word of the whole Christian confession or the whole of Christian dogma. Dogmatics has no more exalted or profound

word—essentially, indeed, it has no other word—than this: that God was in Christ reconciling the world unto himself.[23]

"Dogmatics has ... no other word"! This brings us to the last link between dogs and Christians that I want to mention. And this similarity is related to the fact that ordinarily *dogs don't wear clothes.* Whenever we see dogs with clothes on, we can be sure that this wasn't *their* idea. This, of course, doesn't mean that Christians should likewise run around without clothes on, but it does suggest a very serious problem that churches and Christians have: they wrap themselves up in much too much other stuff just when they should have "no other word." Their problem is their lack of trust in this simple and "central message of the church" that, as Paul put it, in Christ God was reconciling the world to himself, not counting their trespasses against them, and entrusting the message of reconciliation to us. (2 Corinthians 5:19)

Obviously if the Christian good news really boils down to this bite-sized single phrase of "Christ-certified universal salvation"—then the last thing Christians and churches should do is put on so much gear that they can't move. They've fallen hard and *can't get up!* Now they'll have to lie helplessly in one little spot until they freeze to death. In other words, this chronic problem of Christians and churches, and its inevitable solution, look very much like this:

Peanuts, © United Feature Syndicate, Inc.

What do we mean by wearing too much? Bonhoeffer was attempting to answer precisely this question when, in some of the last words he wrote before being murdered by the Gestapo, he struggled with the problem of what the church should look like after the war. For he saw World War II and its devastation as a blown-open doorway to a radical rebirth of the church. What should the church now do? "To make a start," he wrote,

> the church should give away all its property to those in need. The clergy must live solely on the free-will offerings of their congregations, or possibly engage in some secular calling. The church must share in the secular problems of ordinary human life, not dominating, but helping and serving. It must tell men of every calling what it means to live in Christ, to exist for others. In particular ... to take the field against the vices of *hubris*, power-worship, envy, and humbug, as the

roots of all evil. It will have to speak of moderation, purity, trust, loyalty, constancy, patience, discipline, humility, contentment and modesty. It must not under-estimate the importance of human example.... It is not abstract argument, but example, that gives its word emphasis and power.[24]

This is truly a doglike Christian church that Bonhoeffer is advocating, and therefore the true Christian church: humble, poor, loving, faithful, living in fighting trim and solely on the basis of the barest essentials in order to be more effective for its Lord. Churches, like the churches in the New Testament, can be truest to themselves, to others, and to their Lord when they are modest, simple, and small. The dogs of Christ, the churches, should be like a navy's destroyer escorts, the small, lean, and fast warships dedicated specifically to following closely and protecting the really big guns, that being, in this case, "Christ himself, in whom are hidden all the treasures of wisdom and knowledge" (Colossians 2:2–3). Human example can hardly be overestimated, but "dog example" can be a good thing now and then too. And the church should finally get back to being the *type* of dog that it originally was:

Hagar the Horrible, © King Features Syndicate

Unlike the early Christians, with their simple little dog-house-like house churches, today we are no longer mutts. *Where* the early Christians met was unimportant because these mutts themselves were "the church." But today we'd much rather be show dogs, with impressive showplaces for churches and a world of other externals that we have substituted for the internal realities of spirit and understanding. If this is really true of us, then the wide and empty world will have to go on waiting for happiness and healing and the situation will only get worse.

On the other hand, if we do a better job of understanding the secrets of the kingdom of God and sharing these secrets with others, then we will be *real* Christians. And all real

Christians are dogs. We will be what we have been called to be—the faithful and humble and loving servants of our Master—and thus we will be far more effective as healing mirror images of this Master. And that, of course, is why *God* spelled backwards is *dog*.

The churches today and society as a whole (which will always take on the character of the churches' lead) seem to be caught up in little more than the most shallow and missing-the-point concerns and understanding. Therefore, I conclude with the good news enclosed in a home-cooked bite of doggerel, something in the language of the times, which I hope can nevertheless better nourish just by means of this language:

That all are saved is surely and joyfully known
By faithfully following Jesus as Lord alone;
And the way *he* is known is by eating and digesting our
    homework—
The New Testament, God's bare bones.

And so ends my catechism—"the gospel according to dogs."

Notes

1. In discussing the rapid expansion of the early Protestant Reformation in Germany, Roland Bainton, in his famous biography of Luther, tells us, "This success was achieved through a wave of propaganda unequaled hitherto and in its precise form never repeated. The primary tools were the tract and the cartoon" (*Here I Stand: A Life of Martin Luther*, Abingdon Press, 1950, p. 238). This "dog tract" returns to the same technique, and for pretty much the same purposes.

2. The quote is liberally adapted from Bottom in *A Midsummer Night's Dream* V, I, as he attempts to recall what Paul says in 1 Corinthians 2:9.

3. Bainton, *Here I Stand*, p. 284.

4. George Ferguson, *Signs and Symbols in Christian Art*, Oxford University Press, 1959, p. 3.

5. Ferguson, *Signs*, p. 4.

6. *Luther's Works*, vol. 54, *Table Talk*, edited and translated by Theodore Tappert, Fortress Press, 1967, p. 175.

7. Rainer Maria Rilke, quoted in *The Quotable Canine*, edited by Jim Dratfield and Paul Couglin, Doubleday Books, 1995, p. 40.

8. George Graham Vest, quoted in *The Quotable Dog*, edited by George Snider, Contemporary Books, 1994, p. 1.

9. Dietrich Bonhoeffer, *The Cost of Discipleship*, rev. ed., translated by R. H. Fuller, Macmillan, 1963, p. 69.

10. Dietrich Bonhoeffer, *Letters and Papers from Prison*, edited by Eberhard Bethge, translated by Reginald Fuller et al., Simon & Schuster, 1997, pp. 369–70.

11. Quoted in William Barclay, trans., *The Gospel of Luke*, rev. ed., Westminster Press, 1975, p. 77.

12. Tappert, *Luther's Works*, p. 175.

13. *T. S. Eliot: The Complete Poems and Plays*, Harcourt, Brace & Co.,1952, p. 119.

14. Quoted in Bonhoeffer, *The Cost of Discipleship*, p. 277.

15. R. H. McDaniel and Charles H. Gabriel, "Since Jesus Came into My Heart," Copyright 1914 by Charles Gabriel, Rodeheaver Co.

16. Søren Kierkegaard, *Purity of Heart Is to Will One Thing*, translated by D. V. Steere, Harper and Brothers, 1958.

17. Tappert, *Luther's Works*, pp. 37–38.

18. Søren Kierkegaard, *Training in Christianity*, translated by Walter Lowrie, Princeton University Press, 1941, p. 127.

19. Karl Barth, *The Epistle to the Romans*, translated by Edwyn C. Hoskins (London Oxford University Press, 1933), p. 24

20. *Franz Kafka: The Complete Stories,* edited by Nahum N. Glatzer, Schocken Books, 1946, pp. 289–90.

21. Dietrich Bonhoeffer, *Ethics,* translated by Neville Horton Smith, Macmillan, 1965, p. 109.

22. Bonhoeffer, *Ethics,* p. 204 .

23. Karl Barth, *Church Dogmatics,* vol. 11/2, T&T Clark, 1957, p. 88.

24. Dietrich Bonhoeffer, *Letters and Papers from Prison,* edited by Eberhard Bethge, translated by Reginald Fuller et al., Simon & Schuster, 1997, pp. 382–83.

Glossary

Acknowledgments

Permission to reprint the artwork in this volume is gratefully acknowledged to the following:

Rembrandt drawing: *Christ with the Disciples and the Bleeding Woman.* Courtesy of Albertina Vienna.

Overboard © 2003 & 1999 Universal Press Syndicate. Reprinted with permission. All rights reserved.

Pickles © 1999, The Washington Post Writers Group. Reprinted with permission.

Classic Mother Goose & Grimm © GRIMMY, INC. King Features Syndicate. Reprinted with permission.

Mother Goose & Grimm © GRIMMY, INC. King Features Syndicate. Reprinted with permission.

Blondie © King Features Syndicate. Reprinted with permission of Dean Young.

Dog Eat Doug © Brian Anderson and Creators Syndicate, Inc. Reprinted with permission.

Family Circus © Bill Keane, Inc. King Features Syndicate. Reprinted with permission.

115

Bizarro © Dan Piraro. King Features Syndicate. Reprinted with permission.

Hagar the Horrible © King Features Syndicate. Reprinted with permission.

Fred Basset © Solo Syndication. All rights reserved. Reprinted with permission.

Fred Basset © Tribune Media Services, Inc. All rights reserved. Reprinted with permission.

Luann © GEC Inc./Distributed by United Feature Syndicate, Inc.

Peanuts © United Feature Syndicate, Inc.

Dennis the Menace © used by permission of Hank Ketcham Enterprises and © North America Syndicate.

Red and Rover © 2002 The Washington Post Writers Group. Reprinted with permission.

Prickly City © Scott Stantis. Distributed by Universal Press Syndicate. Reprinted with permission. All rights reserved.

Citizen Dog © 1997 Mark O'Hare. Distributed by Universal Press Syndicate. Reprinted with permission. All rights reserved.

Christain Dogma by Karl Bark © Ron Wolfe.

Reprinted with the permission of Scribner, an imprint of Simon & Schuster Adult Publishing Group, from *Letters and Papers from Prison,* edited by Eberhard Bethge, translated by Reginald Fuller et al., Simon & Schuster, 1997.

Photograph credits: iStock/front page, © Stephanie Horrocks; p. 1, © Jim Lim; p. 27, © Fanelie Rosier; p. 40, © Jaimie D. Travis; p. 44, © Michael Chen; p. 64, © Ingvald Kaldhussaeter; p. 73, © Pieter Bregman; p. 106, © Eric Isselée.